OVEREMPLOYED CONFIDENTIAL

Insider Secrets to Make Big F*cking Bucks With Multiple W2 Jobs

by Anonymous in 2022

"Whether you think you can, or you think you can't, you're right."

– Henry Ford

Introduction

It's 10 a.m. on a Friday. I'm sitting in front of three laptops connected to sprawling 32-inch monitors, wearing a "Scrumbag" t-shirt and tighty whities. I'm making a solid $190 an hour as a Senior Project Manager for two different W2 employers, and I still find time to write this book.

How am I able to work two full-time remote jobs in my underwear and write a book at the same time? We will get into that later. For now, just know this isn't some kind of bullshit get-rich-quick hustle. I can't talk about who I am, but I can tell you that I am doing remote work and getting paid a shit-ton of cheese for it. I use Lean practices to avoid wasted time. I am pretty much kick-ass at it.

When I'm in my home office, I don't fuck with social media, I don't chat with my friends, I don't waste time on bullshit work culture events, and I don't take breaks. I work from 8-5 and focus on getting stuff done in the most efficient way possible. I create value for my employers in my underwear. So, while the running underwear undercurrent is some silly bulllshit, creating the home environment to be locked in, and not dilly dally for hours in between projects, is very much fucking serious. If you aren't willing to commit and make a few sacrifices to make this happen, you may as well not read the rest of the book - because that level of attentiveness and conscientiousness is necessary for a bigger bankroll. It demonstrates the level of professionalism and discipline that would command the kind of annual salary we'll be talking about. So while some other strategies discussed here will be multi-step or a sequence of information, this one is simple: don't fucking lolly-gag because those are your hours to figure out your own spectacular technology "I working from home for $500k" solution.

WTF IS OVEREMPLOYED?

How many people do you know with a side hustle? Maybe they do their doodles on Etsy or Uber drunk kids around.d, Por perhaps they serve Mocha Lattes at the local indie coffee shop on weekends. Fuck that. It's mediocre shit money. What if you *have* to pay off medical bills, student loans, or a mortgage, or buy a Ferrari? OverEmployment makes earning this kinda extra money possible for the average wise guy. This book will explain how the concept of overemployment works in practice, divulging insider tips and giving you the tools to optimize your performance while raking in the big bucks from two or three remote jobs.

'OverEmployed' is when you work two /*or more*/ full-time remote jobs simultaneously, during the same hours. Typically, this happens without either of the employers' knowledge - because they are not on a "need-to-know" basis if you cover your bases! e. OverEmployment allows crafty workers to double or triple their salaries and *still* work an 8-10 hour schedule. It takes organization, smarts, and cast iron balls. Prepare to forge yours while turning these pages.

The pandemic's lingering effects on office ecosystems can be summarized as this: remote workers have become the standard for day-to-day operations. Since the pandemic began, working remotely has become a new standard for technology workers. Working outside their manager's direct line of sight has permitted employees to take additional W2 jobs during the regular workday. Think about how much time you spend doing *real* work in an average workday. OverEmployment asks that you measure how much "downtime" you have when on-site at a single technology gig. You have to admit there is a lot of downtime, right? Maybe you browse Facebook or do a little shopping? Or, perhaps you're killing some time jerkin' to Pornhub while the old mouse jiggler keeps you active on Slack? Point is, you probably find yourself sitting on your hands a lot - unless you're doing the last option, in which case your hands are probably always active.

OverEmployment is about utilizing that extra time to take on another full-time W2 gig and double your income. YES, straight up, DOUBLE your income. But, no more jerking it at work. Please, for the love of all that is green like money and holy.

The insider tips in this book allow workers to maximize the number of paychecks they receive while minimizing time devoted to each W2. Sometimes, people hold down three or four jobs and make high six figures. Keep reading to learn how to measure downtime at each possible technology gig, and build up a system that allows you to contribute to each company *without sacrificing all your time and efforts to any single one.* Capitalizing on "downtime" by leveraging remote working environments is at the core of OverEmployment. To do it correctly, you need a proper blueprint for preparation - consider this book a guide for exactly that: how to turn your monolithic technology working schedule into a scaled-and-optimized microservices infrastructure... ;).

/*Anonymous*/ Sr. Engineering Manager with 10+ years of experience killing it with four

jobs. His total base is around $670k with small sign-on bonuses from jobs 3 & 4.

HAVE THE POWER HE-MAN

Traditionally, the American workforce model pushes one-sided loyalty from the worker to the company. You're supposed to feel like you owe them all your life's work hours, grinding soul for allowing you to work daily to improve their business and line their maladjusted asshole pockets with profits. Unfortunately, this sense of obligation often keeps you from earning your full potential. That, or the fear of reprisals from your employer (more on how to handle contract details and non-compete/non-disclosure Agreements). As a result, workers get brainwashed into staying with one employer who "did so much for you." Yet, the same company will lay that person off as soon as the numbers dictate it is better for their bottom line.

If they operate in that matter - like a cutthroat financial corporate raider - then you should, too.

These Orwellian organizations recruit technology workers in droves because technology work is a very specific, essential niche of "know-how" knowledge: technology workers can do something their companies cannot. You know how to do something that they can't do, and technology workers enjoy (generally) higher base pay because they're paying you well. After all, it's not easy to find people that know what is needed to resolve all issues related to computer infrastructure. you know. Your fucking brain and spindly technology fingers are an asset in a free-market economy after all! It's your golden ticket. The law of supply and demand dictates that you should get as much money for that hard-earned braininess as the market will bear. Because the demand for these technical skills is higher than the supply - especially with so many companies either moving to digital infrastructure or fully incorporating remote tech - technology workers have an opportunity to maximize their financial leverage through remote OverEmployment.

OverEmployment critics have claimed that having multiple jobs secretly is unethical or could be considered theft. To all detractors asshats, I pose a question:

Do you like apples? Also, fuck you.

If you're growing some amazing apples and selling them on the side of the road, and you can sell two apples at once to two different customers, is that considered theft? Your customers are satisfied because the apples are delicious and rare, and it's not your fault that you're efficient and able to sell two apples at once. It shouldn't matter as long as the customers get the service they expect and the product is good. Each technology problem you resolve is just another apple sold. How do you like them apples?

In knowledge work, we are not wage slaves. We are not riding the clock until the end of each day to go home and forget all about it. We are tasked, each day, with creating value by solving complex problems. Valuable that the employer will turn around and sell it as a product, like an apple. Who knows, they may even be selling it to *two* customers at once. Don't get me wrong; I am not complaining about capitalism; to the contrary, I love it, love it, love it. We just need not forget that it works *both* ways. You are a business. Act accordingly.

/*Anonymous*/ He's an information security engineer who always makes sure he has cash flow redundancy. He's been three-job hustling for the last four years for $500k+.

REVENGE OF THE NERD

IT jobs are perfect for OverEmployment because you can do most technology jobs anywhere. In addition, technology jobs are in demand and pay well, so if you want to maximize your income, technology is a great place to do it. Even learning some basic technology skills, getting important certifications, or growing the skill level of your current ability all have wonderful payoffs on the side - makes the grass greener.

In the current environment, OverEmployment doesn't seem too big of a deal to employers. I've never heard an employer complain about a developer creating value with their excellent work and thus making clients happy - all while on their clock... Imagine a VP saying, "you're brilliant and delivering great work, and we have to let you go because you're sharing your brain with other people, and that makes us super jealous." Keep reading to find out how to earn the respect of execs and managers you interact with in the professional space, empowering your schedule by making any other employment info about you on a "need-to-know" basis.

Good developers, project managers, and DevOps people are hard to find - certainly not a dime a dozen. Once someone lands a truly competent technology worker (hopefully you), you and you're doing a good job, they will overlook a lot to keep you around. So why not own the opportunity and make what you deserve?

/*Anonymous*/ Cloud architect who couldn't decide between two offers took both! Then came the biggest surprise: after he started the two careers, he

got an offer from Facebook. So now he's doing all three positions and making $485K annually.

THE BIG BUCKS

Okay, so now let's get to the greenery shit. First, let's give a ballpark range for the annual salary and the kind of money to generally expect on the job. Let's take one job that has 3 hours of intensive labor, and 6 hours of downtime, and instead use OverEmployment to work remote for those 3 intensive hours, then pick up two other full-time jobs that have a similar flow of "as-needed" technology work:

, I suppose you want to know how much money we're talking about. I'm sure you have some idea based on your income and some basic math, but it doesn't hit you until you see those paychecks go into your bank account and realize that you're making $30,000 a month. That's a significant number and not unusual. Some people are making double that.

$125,000 + $125,000 + $125,000 = $375,000 or $31,250 per month.

Let's take another example: You're making $125,000, living on $75,000, and saving $50,000 a year. At that rate, it will take you twenty years to save $1,000,000. Saving $1,000,000 in 20 years is a fan-fucking-tastic accomplishment. You'll probably be able to rent a jet ski and maybe an AirBnB for the summer!

Now, let's pretend you have three jobs that pay $125,000 a year. You live comfortably on $175,000 and save $200,000 a year. At that rate, you can reach $1,000,000 in savings in only five years. And, you still get to party like a rock star on $175,000 a year! Naked sushi. Strippers. And you OWN the AirBnB vacation home that the other guy, working mindlessly picking his nose during the downtime at a single gig, has to rent from you. That's the difference between a technology worker who leverages "OverEmployment." The OverEmployment individual gauges "downtime vs. as-needed" activity for each position, maximizes his time earned, and OWNS instead of rents. That's what is at stake when considering your streams of income. Note that I said streams - plural. Don't limit your talents to just one employer, even if the other jobs are just side gigs. If you want to take it to the next level and make full-time money while doing fulfilling tech work all day long, then OverEmployment empowers you to even take on other W-2 full-time positions. All your employers are happy, and you are AT LEAST three times as happy... but that happiness, like money, has the potential to compound over time. So, keep all that in mind while strategizing your very own OverEmployment technology solution..

After five years, you can smoke weed in every coffee bar across AmsterdamEurope. Maybe you want to go back to one job and take it easy, or keep piling those fat stacks and work two or three jobs. The point is, in five years, you can relax and do whatever you want - a digital nomad by choice - because you have a good chunk of savings to fall back on. Let me say that again, *five years*. That's all it takes to save $1,000,000. What did you do over the last five years, and where did it get you?

/*Anonymous*/ She's in analytics and a single mom hustling for her baby. After taking on a second job, she landed another full-time offer and is planning to work all three jobs while weighing which of the jobs to keep. She stands to make $23k this month.

INSIDER SECRETS

Okay! Here's the book part where the OverEmployment blueprint comes alive. The following chapters cover this where you learn the nuts and bolts of OverEmployment, how to pull it off, and what experienced people have learned. Hopefully, this information will help you avoid the pitfalls and achieve 2x or 3x income.

/*Anonymous*/ He's been living the OverEmployed life for eight months with jobs one and two. January bonuses were paid out, and he made 20% on top of base salaries, which were over $25K per month. Best January ever.

Chapter 1

Getting The Jobs

There is no such thing as a no-sale call. A sale is made on every call you make. Either you sell the client...or he sells you. The only question is who is gonna close? You or him? ~ Ben Affleck, Boiler Room, 2000

This book is not about interviews - you should have already prepped some interview skills when getting your first job! This book is about the next step: overemployment. And with that caveat, adjusting and angling your interview technique becomes necessary for a smooth OverEmployment operation. Now, someone walks away from every interview a winner. You need to decide if it is going to be you. In the technology industry, I can leave a job and guarantee another job offer within two weeks because I carefully curate my resume and present myself well during interviews. Below are a few things that work for me, along with other valuable multi-job hunting tips:

MISE EN SCÈNE

Fulling a specific role and vision in these people's minds. You can be different when the work camera is off, but remember you are presenting your brand when talking to them. You are playing the ROLE OF technology PERSON for this company - that's it. If that is the only dimension of you the company ever saw, and you performed well during it, they'd be overjoyed bringing you aboard. Don't feel like you have to reinvent the wheel during an interview. There is a spot to fill, so remember while on camera that you are, to a large degree, demonstrating your ability to play that work role in social and business environments.

With that said, imagine that the remote work camera is your place to make a strong, well-defined first impression. You need to make sure your set pieces (your background) and your actors (you) are ready and set to perform.

For example, I imagine what I would want to see in a truly ideal technology partner; someone that I'd breathe a sigh of relief and say, "This dude is amazing at his job." I go in and aim to be that person to my prospective employers during interviews. You must think about every aspect of the impression you make in these sessions. It is not just about your skills.

I set my office up like a little studio, with a backdrop that shows a shade of personality: a drumset in the corner, carefully selected art, and some records stacked on a 60s Pioneer speaker. I even set up lighting to make everything look perfect through the camera itself. Overhead lighting sucks - think like an amateur photographer... and not a shitty one! I directionally light everything as if I intend to film a movie. I light the drum set from the bottom to make it glow, and I'll throw cool shadows on the wall. I also light my framed original art. (Posters are not art.) I'm trying to convey class, style, and general awesomeness. Be prepared to talk about things in your staged backdrop that kick-ass details about you. A detail like well-framed, tasteful, art illuminated on the wall can elicit the kind of split-second first impression that makes potential employers go, "Oh, well I already like this guy, let's see if he knows anything about the kind of role we're trying to fill at the company."

For my face, I use a warming 13-inch ring light. And I dress impeccably, but not too formal. Just neat and slightly stylish. Make it appear like you are about 5-10% more casual, but you could be ready to shave and go to the office in a half hour if needed. In the past, I used standalone webcams so I could position them perfectly to capture my best angle. However, now I stick to the built-in laptop cameras and mics to avoid technical glitches with drivers and switching across Zoom, Teams, and Google Meet applications. Glitches with your audio or camera make you look incompetent. Has that shit nailed by testing thoroughly? If you are sharing, share the window BEFORE they get on the call. Share the window, not the whole screen, so your buddy messaging you leaked celebrity porn won't pop up in their view. If you can't get that conference call right, how can they expect you to deliver defect-free code?

All this may sound a bit contrived, and truthfully that is ok - this is a job interview, not your interview with God. Don't leave anything to chance during these job interviews. Remember, you have already established a single job; this interview is angling to go for 2 or even three w-2 positions. Blueprinting your maneuvers from the interview will ensure you stay in control even while juggling multiple positions for multiplied pay. I don't want my interviewer distracted by how sallow I look, or how my nasty office looks like I just had the world's lamest bender. I will not use a fake background and give the impression that I'm hiding my loser-ass crib. I want them to want to be me. I want to convey I have 100% of my shit together. Perception is reality. Think crisp, and well-defined, and stage your best set pieces to appear "in your element" while interviewing!

BE READY FOR ANYTHING

Looking good means reflecting on if you come across as a dumbass. Do your due diligence—research the company's history and what they do. Research your interviewers on Linked in and find ways to identify with them.

Smile and make small talk. Try to get them talking about themselves. And if they do start telling you about their pet or kids, DO NOT try to take back the conversation or talk about your pet without them directly asking. You win if you can get through an entire interview with the interviewer talking about themselves the whole time. They will walk about thinking about how much they like you and have no idea why.

Be a subject matter expert. Look up common questions for your field and have good answers ready. Keep cheat sheets on your desk but out of view of the camera. Be prepared to tell a story about a success, a failure, and an event that changed you. And, for Christ's sake, know how to answer the "What is your greatest weakness?" question. Hint: It's nooooooot that you care too much, or that your talents are misunderstood, ok?

All of this assumes that you are a complete and total badass at whatever it is you do. If you can't do the job, don't waste your time on an interview. Instead, spend time honing your skills.

YOU ARE A BUSINESS

OverEmployment fosters a savvy business mind. Remember you're committing to solve twice as many problems in the same amount of time /*which is not unusual for a pushy employer to ask of you.*/ However, you're doing it for yourself across multiple jobs and getting paid for the extra effort. Think of yourself as a business trying to maximize your profits.

You never know when an opportunity will end, so it's best to keep interviewing, looking for new possibilities, and keeping your skills sharp when you're forced to go out and find a new job. I recommend interviewing for at least one job a month to stay sharp and explore new possibilities.

JOB TWO INTERVIEW

Approach the "job two" interview like any other interview. If an interviewer asks whether you have another full-time job, you don't have to lie. You can say that you have a full-time job, and give a good reason why you are looking for a new one. You can offer to show them pay stubs from a start date and the most recent pay period if they require proof of employment. /***Just don't say that you don't plan on quitting that current job.*/ You can say you are "looking for something new," or are trying to "expand your horizons," or whatever - but don't mention your plan to stay. As**

long as you read the rest of this ebook, it won't matter to them, nor be any of their business.

If I'm leaving a job, I usually get contact info from someone I'm tight with, and I ask to use them as a reference down the road. Of course, I offer to trade the favor. Let your references know when someone might be calling about you and coach them on what to say. Don't tell the reference you're working multiple jobs. Just let them know what you're applying for and the details you want them to reveal about you. In other words, be specific, so the reference feels it's easy to respond with what they've prepped, and the call goes on without a hitch or any room for misinterpretation.

A BACKUP RESUME

I keep two versions of my resume ready at any time. For example, I'm a senior-level manager, but suppose I'm applying for a job that is a junior-level position in a bid to take on less responsibility. In that case, I will use the pared-down version of my resume because my primary resume is too loaded.

If you're applying for job number three, you may want a job that allows you to take it a little easier. A junior-level position can let you play a little clueless when you need extra time in your schedule. It pays less, but if it's your third salary, what does $12,000 matter?

Using an alternate resume might mean leaving out some of your past jobs, but it doesn't mean you should lie to pad your resume. Lies are hard to remember and may be revealed during a background check. You can even mention the same companies, but have fun doing the reverse of normal resume building: play DOWN your accomplishments, not up. That way, your second and/or third OverEmployment positions do not feel as intensive or hectic as the first one.

STARTUPS OR BOOMERS

When choosing whether I want to work at a startup or a more established Baby Boomer company, I look at the culture, aims, and day-to-day operation of the company. Startups are typically considered bad for OverEmployment because they generally require short deadlines in overzealous business culture. Startups may want you to commit to them on a "devoted minion" level - not compatible with OverEmployment. So, while a new tech startup environment can be inspiring, it is probably not the place for OverEmployment's salary-maximizing strategy.

Boomer companies may be settled into a particular way of doing things and offer a calmer environment. However, you can get derailed by detailed background searches or bogged down in bureaucracy that requires extra work and doesn't necessarily produce anything. Make sure you're able to sniff this shit a mile away, or you'll find yourself wasting all your "downtime" in dreaded meetings that go nowhere.

I prefer to work at Boomer companies with a matrix management structure. In matrix management, things move slowly, and several layers of people perform different tasks on the same project. . For example, in a start-up, I act simultaneously as the Scrum Master, Product Owner, and Project Manager on a project. While in a larger company, I may be the Project Manager with a separate Scrum Master and Product Owner on my team. My workload is much lighter, and I have people to cover for me if I miss an event.

These are scenarios based on my experience; every place is different, and candidates must examine them on a case-by-case basis. When you start interviewing with a new business, you must do your background research and learn as much as possible about the organization's internal management structure and employee policies. Ask many questions; even if the answers are not entirely forthcoming, the interviewer's reaction will often tell you what you need to know.

OFFSHORE OUTSIDER

If you're considering a second or third job in another country, you should consider several things.

The most obvious impediment is the language barrier. If you're looking to take a job in a foreign country, you likely already have a plan; you may be bilingual. In this scenario, use different computers for each new job. Your language settings will differ on each computer, so it should help mitigate mix-ups as long as you speak both languages. I wouldn't recommend working in a situation where companies list translating with software as a prerequisite for hire. It'll be more time-consuming, your work will be less efficient, and your bottom line will suffer. Remember, you are a business; efficiency means more money. Learn to play the role of "excellent technology guy" in each of these organizations, and remember that may not look the same. Let any time zone differences remind you how much the success of OverEmployment hinges on flexibility and adaptability,

Working in different countries typically means working in different time zones. As a result, you could find yourself working on a more extended schedule. For example, it might not be sustainable if you are based in the US and working with a seven-hour time difference in Europe for your second job. The goal is to perform the jobs at the same timebox as one typical job. Unless you're willing to wake up and work a shift at 3 AM, you'll want to carefully consider time zones when picking what positions to stack for your OverEmployment strategy.

If you decide to work in a foreign country, try to get something within a few hours of your time zone. One or two hours staggered is ideal because it gives you extra time to focus on the new job without getting too far outside your regular work schedule.

Foreign countries have different tax laws. While this problem can be mitigated, the solutions will be at the cost of your time and emotional bandwidth. Moreover, just because it can be dealt with doesn't necessarily mean it's a good idea. If you want to keep it simple, avoid working in multiple countries. If you're considering it anyway, consult a tax attorney, and fuck off for not listening to my advice. We are trying to turn a tanker here!

Work cultures will differ significantly from one country to the next. Some places may require more communication and hand-holding than others. Some places don't use deodorant. If you're not familiar with the culture of the country where you intend to work, I suggest staying the hell away. The longer it takes to acclimate to a different culture, the less money you're making—the time spent trying to fit in will limit your ability to work more jobs.

TIME TIME ZONES

Time zones can be your friend when working multiple jobs in the United States. Living in Central time, I prefer working one job in Eastern time and one in Western time. I can spend mornings working on the East coast job, knowing I have three hours before the West coast job comes online.

If I have something important to finish for the West Coast client, I can work late with some quiet time after the East Coast goes offline. It also helps free up my meeting times when I can schedule East Coast in the morning and West Coast in the afternoon.

The different lunch hours give me two open blocks of time in the middle of the day when I know one company will not schedule meetings. These little differences make two jobs' worth of meetings far more manageable. I have three round clocks on the wall, each with a different timezone and labels of East, Central, and West. They are helpful, and they look awesome. It appears 1-4 hour time differences are a sweet spot for time zone differences between OverEmployment positions.

One more note about time zones: I hate to stereotype, but people on the West Coast are humorless, people in the Northeast are assholes, and people in the South, while friendly, will talk about the weather endlessly. Pick your poison. You'll be able to gleefully ignore all of it with the 2x salary.

CHECKING YOUR RAP SHEET

Background checks validate your education, criminal record, addresses, and other public records. From time to time, you might get an employer that uses Work Number Employment

Data. A Work Number is a record that provides employment and income information(*This number is a creation of Equifax.) It includes data collected from employers and large sector payroll processors about your past employment and income information. The good news is you can freeze your Work Number Employment Data with a few simple steps. (*More information is provided in the next section).

It's unusual for a company to run a background check on an existing employee. The exception is if you're in an industry that puts you in a sensitive or secure role where compliance is an issue. For example, a role in the federal government may require regular background checks. However, most commercial tech jobs don't give a shit.

YOU CAN FREEZE YOUR RECORDS

An Equifax Work Number records your employment and income information; it includes data collected from employers and large payroll processors.

Freeze your employment data by going onto the Equifax site and requesting a freeze on information related to your work number. This seemingly insignificant errand is a safety net just in case an employer does a check with Equifax.

You can prevent access to your employment information with an employment data freeze:

- A freeze is free to place or remove.

- Verifiers cannot view your Work Number data if you place a freeze.

- If you want your information to be accessible to certain third parties, you will need to remove the freeze.

To request a freeze via email, write to: TWNFreeze@equifax.com requesting a "Freeze Placement Form."

A Freeze Placement Form will be sent with a secure email feature to complete the process. It's a pretty simple form and doesn't cost anything to submit.

https://employees.theworknumber.com/employee-data-freeze

PICK A DAMN JOB

While OverEmployment advocates finding other W-2 positions that fit in the schedule, those second and third occupations come after your primary job: the job around which your entire strategy revolves. You keep the primary job golden, free of drama, and full of great performance reviews, and the other two jobs can more casually revolve at your discretion. Determine which job is your primary job, and make sure you protect it. This job is your primary source of income and medical benefits. Your other jobs are considered "burners," or jobs you are not attached to and can leave anytime. They're disposable and replaceable like a burner phone. If you lose a burner job, don't sweat it, it just means the possibility of a new job that pays better just presented itself. Your primary job is your fallback. It's the job that you protect so you can pay the bills if everything else goes wrong.

DON'T SIGN SHIT

Both jobs will likely be in the same field simply because you are highly kick-ass in that discipline. However, in some situations, you'll be asked to sign a non-disclosure agreement (NDA) or non-compete that prevents you from working in other jobs in the same field. It's important to honor any non-compete agreement that you have signed. These are enforceable contracts, and they're not a joke. Don't sign any overly aggressive non-compete. If they try to press it, say, "fuck off," and get on to the next job. If you are still considering a position requiring an NDA or non-compete, be sure to have your lawyer review it for potential conflicts. In other words, when you are handed a "non-compete" clause, "Non-Disclosure agreement," or a similar document, pause and wait to sign until you have cleared its stipulations, and how they could impact your OverEmployment.

Chapter 2

Manage The Jobs

GET ON BOARD

Onboarding a new job can be exhausting. You have to learn all the new names and quirks of what people do in each workspace and navigate the politics of each new company. Try to keep a job long enough to pay for the agony it takes to onboard. I recommend keeping each job for a minimum of six months to a year. That said, If you are miserable, fuck it. Walk out. Or sign off.

BAD SECURITY

Use one password for all work computers and software if you can get away with it. I typically use one complex password and change it across all devices when forced to make a password change. This practice is antithetical to security, but in multiple employment, you end up with several systems and machines that require different passwords. You don't want to look like an asshole by getting locked out of your computers all the time. Many companies will use services for password storage, but the solutions are often different from place to place. Having one password to get you in and out quickly is easier. /*Note: keep your shit off those machines since they are insecure as fuck due to your one-password strategy.*/

MF'n MFA

I recommend keeping multi-factor authentication apps for each job on different phones. You can use an old phone or buy a cheap one, and you don't have to get a data plan. Simply connect the phone to your Wi-Fi, and install the 2FA apps. Keeping the jobs separate will save your sanity in the long run.

CROSS-CONTAMINATION

This step is crucial. Do not mix your job hardware. Use each laptop you're given for the intended job and don't try to use one machine for multiple jobs. Ever. If you are not given laptops, then buy one for each job. Don't be a cheap bastard.

Each machine is the physical embodiment of the workplace and will save you from sending the wrong message to the wrong person at the wrong company. Also, you never know when a nosy technology guy will be poking around on the company computer to see what you are up to. These little precautions listed all add up to airtight security as you glide from position to position.

CAMERAS OFF

Given what you're trying to accomplish by holding multiple jobs simultaneously, meetings requiring cameras are a pain in the ass. As a project manager, I have the luxury of setting a precedent on whether or not a meeting requires video. Some companies have policies dictating cameras to be on during specific events. Others are decided on an ad-hoc basis. If you're in a situation where you have the choice, always have the camera off. Do this to set the expectation for when you must have it off for a double meeting session.

ASS KISSER

Set realistic expectations with your manager that you can guarantee to meet. Communicate early and often, such as reporting to stakeholders before you are asked. Send weekly updates to your supervisor, even if it's just to say you're continuing work on something. **These proactive efforts may keep him from micromanaging you.** Finally, always say "yes" even if you have to say yes to something you know will find a way to get out of it down the road. In other words, kiss a little ass for the greater goal. This part of of the strategy involves some social acuity, so don't be a jackass or act haughty to your manager; they'll likely sniff out your dumb ploys at that point.

DUH

Hopefully, you can think on your feet, but if you can't, create a list of ready-made questions and answers for any situation. For example, in a development meeting, you can almost always say, "Will it scale?" and be perceived as intelligent and thoughtful. Have a sheet developed of a "go-to" back of rhetorical tricks that don't interrupt anyone else's train of thought in the meeting, but don't necessarily take that much engagement to remark on. For example, by asking, "Hmm, how will it scale?" You give the impression the whole time you were quiet because you were thinking about approaches to scalability - not because you were finishing a coding system for a different project.

FUCKING INTERNET

Don't underestimate the power of blaming the fucking internet. If you find yourself on a call when someone mentions your name, and you aren't paying attention, simply say, "Fucking internet. Could you repeat the question?" It sounds a lot better than saying, "Uhhh, I wasn't paying attention. What were you talking about?" And everyone has a problem, so no one's going to debate whether you're a liar. At the same time, if it becomes a regular occurrence, you'll be the technology guy that can even handle his fucking internet. So, use this excuse as a red-alert, when you feel caught off-guard and obligated to respond to something.

TO-DO TO-DON'T

Take lots of notes, and keep a to-do list for each job. I keep a separate laptop open, logged into my personal Google account, with a Google doc for daily notes on all projects. This is my consolidation point for notes, so I have them saved on my account if I lose access to one of my work computers. Like, say, if I get fired. I use Google Tasks within each company's Google account for to-do lists. That way, I can be 100% engaged, take 100% engaged notes, then totally drop the task for that moment, and move on. Later, when I pick the notes back up, I can quickly return to 100% engagement. Keep this aim in mind when organizing your OverEmployment work schedule.

Chapter 3

Maximize Efficiency

DO AS LITTLE AS POSSIBLE

"Simplicity is the art of maximizing the work not done" is an Agile principle central to OverEmployment. To make your process more sustainable, you must do less. Paring down your practices to the responsible essentials, and removing bottlenecks, lets you travel light. Save your emotional bandwidth by minimizing wasted time and improving your ability to focus on the most critical issues. That sounded new-age douchy, but it's real. Lean thinking is the truth. Lean Startup and Design Thinking Principles can help ensure you have optimized your OverEmployment schedule efficiency.

DEEP BRAIN

Multitasking during deep brain thinking is inefficient and should be avoided. I would consider complex tasks such as writing code, DevOps infrastructure development, creative problem solving, and Wordle to be tasks where multitasking is counterproductive. For any task where you feel you are using your judgment, skills, and critical thinking to "bring multiple pieces together," avoid multitasking. Your brain wants and needs to focus on not fraying during higher-order tasks.

In these situations, context switching can reduce productivity by as much as 40%. This is because your brain has to reorient itself each time you switch focus. It requires time and effort to return to its previous state on a complex problem. You have to think your way back to where you left off.

Notes can help re-enter that area, but they cannot replicate the fluid state of

Multitasking is fine for dipshit tasks like processing emails, video conferences, listening to music, eating, answering phones, and data entry. However, multitasking is advantageous for non-critical tasks using visual, audio, and motor skills. For example, multitasking is fantastic when simultaneously smoking weed while watching The Wizard of Oz and listening to Pink Floyd's Dark Side of the Moon.

YODA SHIT

If you can learn to be present in two to three meetings simultaneously, you will find that it is an invaluable skill to make OverEmployment succeed. When I say be present, I mean following the thread of two conversations simultaneously. To do it, you have two earbuds for two of the conversations, with one in each ear.

This is a pretty advanced skill that I have not yet mastered—some real Yoda shit. I have to more or less tune out the non-active conversations. I usually keep my main meeting set at a medium volume while turning the others down low enough that I don't hear what they're saying, but I can recognize if my name is called. And, when I jump back in, I say, "sorry, fucking internet." I will say, it may be a theoretical technique, because the level of balancing here may just not be worth the effort on a day-to-day basis. Don't overcomplicate the situation, and do your best to have some meetings with no camera, or only over chat/text. The fewer meetings you can prove you don't need to be involved in off the bat, the better. To them, you can be the weird-yet-effective technology who hangs out in the basement. The less attention the better.

MEDIOCRACY

That may sound like a shit thing, particularly when you have to be a genius to pull off what I describe in this book. But, unfortunately, you will have to rein yourself in when your instincts tell you to dominate. It's unnatural for most of us and can be hard to stomach, but just think about the fat stacks going into your bank account and suck it up.

Being mediocre means you do a good job but don't stand out because you will be given more work and responsibility if you stand out. So, don't go winning any awards, or you'll be asked to lead guilds and host stupid events. Oh, and remember, "Next Friday Is Hawaiian Shirt Day!"

Keeping your schedule as simple as possible means no extracurricular shit. Be the dull, quiet guy in meetings. Keep your head down and do good work while drawing as little attention as possible.

It can be pretty embarrassing to be a slacker when you know you're capable of much more. But, unfortunately, it's part of the game. Channel that inner go-getter to moderate success collecting extraordinary paychecks, instead of extraordinary performance at a single job for a paltry paycheck. So, when you're embarrassed by your mediocre performance review, just think about the double or triple salary, and you'll feel better.

STAY ON TARGET

OverEmployment is about focus and efficiency. Working multiple jobs requires agility and quick thinking on your feet. To ensure I get my work done, I block off focus time and try to group similar tasks to work on during that time. Anything that I can delegate to my virtual assistant, I pass off to him. If a job requires deep thinking, I make sure I have this time to minimize context switching.

I GOT BETTER SHIT TO DO

Block off all of your calendars for critical recurring meetings. For example, if job one requires you to do scrum stand-ups every day at 11 a.m., block off that time across your calendars. Do this for all important recurring meetings. Sometimes it can be tricky balancing the schedule without blocking off too much in other job calendars. It looks fishy if your *job one* calendar is full and there are no *job one* meetings.

This is where using different time zones and scheduling recurring meetings at lunch in different time zones can be helpful. For example, if you have to schedule recurring Zooms in *job one* on the East Coast, schedule them in the morning when *job two* on the West coast has not come online yet. And vice versa, you can plan your recurring meetings for your career too late in the afternoon after *job one* has gone offline.

This is not a foolproof plan; you'll often have to think on your feet to explain why you need to block off a recurring time. For example, my jobs believe that all my kids are in therapy, so I have to go to regularly scheduled appointments for three different kids three times a week. It's a little awkward, but it's a great excuse.

You should also block off time for focused work. Focused work blocks can be used across all of your calendars at the same time so you can focus on results for whatever jobs require them at that time.

ROBO CALENDAR

Calendar automation is fucking killer. You use a calendar consolidation tool to allow you to view your schedules and several different companies on one calendar. It gives a simple visual representation of potential overlaps and problems in your scheduling across other companies. Several various services offer calendar automation tools. They are critical in managing complex schedules. Below I've listed some examples of calendar tools:

- ClockWise
- MixMax
- CalendarBridge
- Calendly

I keep a personal laptop open and log into my personal Google account and use this to run my Calendar Automation software. It displays on a 42" TV on the wall and is an information radiator for my entire schedule.

SKIP THAT SHIT

All-hands, town halls, optional training, virtual game nights, and culture guilds are all bullshit Kool-Aid drinking sessions. Community meetings are a waste of time. l always try to get out of them if my boss is not there.

If you want to stay off the radar and not be that person who always misses community meetings, show up early and give facetime for a few minutes as an "establishing shot," then turn off the tape and mute the audio. Then, you can let it play in the background while you move on to something more important. At the same time, you can still keep tabs on the meeting should your input truly be required for the successful project.

If a community meeting is essential, someone will take notes or record the session and send it out later. You can watch it, fast through the boring parts, and note the essential elements. Or even better, you can have your assistant do it and give you notes on the salient points. Always ask to have these notes sent out, or, better yet, record them yourself should you find yourself missing crucial elements at key points in the meeting!

Chapter 4

Save Your Sanity

WHAT THE HELL DO YOU WANT?

Go into each job with a goal and regularly remind yourself of that goal. What purpose does this particular position play in the grander scheme of your plans for the year? For the next 3 years? 5 years? Then, write down what you need from the job to achieve your goal, and give it a timeframe. If you're indecisive and don't focus on the goal, it's a recipe for failure, burnout, and termination. Work toward a fixed goal, and get the hell out of Dodge when the time is right.

FORGET IT

If possible, take a couple of days off while you get adjusted. However, I recommend taking at least a whole week off. Most orientations for remote work involve briefings and get-to-know-you sessions /*depending on the culture of your job two company*/, and it's essential to make great first impressions by being present. It's also an excellent opportunity to learn more about the expectations so you can ramp up and kick ass accordingly.

When onboarding job two, plan out in advance how to take some time off from job one. Ideally, pick the "down season" for your line of work, and also look to use sick pay or a couple of vacation days. You are going to want entire days to enjoy shifting into "2nd" and "3rd" gear for your OverEmployment positions. The most stressful time at most jobs is the first couple weeks of orientation, so keep that in mind when officially stacking positions on top of each other. When you're getting to know your coworkers, learning your way around the interdepartmental systems, dealing with all the new rules and regulations, and comprehending what you're supposed to be doing from day to day in your job, this is when you do not want distractions from other jobs. Otherwise, the stress can be too much and make the situation untenable. Plan to take some vacation for the first week or two of your onboarding at the new job.

FUCK NO, I WON'T GO

Be willing to say, "I can't make that meeting," or better yet, shed your pusillanimous worker skin and tell the truth with, "this meeting is a waste of my time." No one is going to argue with your assertiveness. Most people don't want conflict. They just want to do the bare minimum to get through the day so they can go home, order pizza, and watch some Succession. And marry a stripper. But being real, test if the company is ok with you being a bit standoffish and bristly when it comes to your time. If you do great work for two weeks, then suddenly are called into a meeting you believe will cause a scheduling conflict, try being as straightforward as the following sample email:

> "These technology systems are delicate, and I do not have time for meetings unless there is something urgent, or a mistake I made needs to be addressed right away. Otherwise, I prefer not to attend meetings and gatherings, as it disrupts my focus on the granular details of technology server maintenance."

If you get back a response to the effect of, "Woah, ok lone cowboy, just keep doing a great job... we'll keep the contact to a minimum so long as you keep nailing your role here," then you have found a keeper for OverEmployment. If you get the sense the boss is a working stiff claiming, "I'm sorry, but meetings are mandatory, and you have to be there just cause," it doesn't matter if the salary is great, or the actual technical aspects of the job are easy. It's time to bounce. These random meetings are the kind of time-sappers that make lucrative OverEmployment opportunities impossible.

MAKE technology RAIN

This one sounds like a no-brainer, but it is easier said than done. Make sure you use all of your available vacation time. You don't want to leave a job and leave money on the table. Instead, enjoy your life while you sit on a beach and get paid thousands of dollars to do *shit*. In other words, go to work when you're a little sick, and only skip if you are so ill, it will make you fuck up while on the job. That way, you hopefully have some vacation days stocked up for either a blowout vacation or flexibility in adjusting to new OverEmployment opportunities.

GET A LITTLE HELP

I have an assistant with extensive experience in HR and occupational psychology that submits job applications for me, does spreadsheet work, takes notes on long discovery videos, and does other time-consuming tasks related to my jobs. He is more intelligent and educated than me, and the fact I can delegate these kinds of tasks, which otherwise would take me a day of hair-pulling stress for a mediocre result, is fantastic.

HABITUAL LINE STEPPERS

A critical aspect of OverEmployment is setting boundaries with your employers and co-workers. Be strong, set rigid boundaries, and only be flexible when necessary. If you do this from the outset, people will see it as part of your personality, not as trying to get away with something.

It's important to create routines for yourself, so you have the structure that will help you avoid making mistakes.

- Every morning look at your calendar and think about how you will get through your schedule that day.

- Schedule breaks. Kids are a good excuse when you must find a reason to step away from the keyboard. Probe where you can develop the rhythm of leaving for something necessary where colleagues and management seemingly could care less. If you feel something important, and like the team is secretly counting on you to keep pulling your weight, note how often you feel you cannot step away from the keyboard for even a minute. That could cause an immediate issue with other employers.

- When you leave your keyboard at the end of the day, leave your keyboard and don't come back. It's important to create a separation between your job and free time. Because there will be a lot of clearly defined work... so balance it with clearly-defined fun time :)

- Find a way to wind down that doesn't involve your computer. This is different for everyone. You may go for a run, visit some friends, hit the bar, or just watch a movie or read a book, but the key is to refresh your brain, take a break from the computer, and distract yourself so you can be fresh for the next day's work. Any y activity besides more web surfing is highly recommended for some semblance of a balanced life

- Stick to your boundaries even when it comes to your boss.

SLOW YOUR ROLL

Do not fall for the seductive siren song of multiple offers. ever try to onboard two jobs simultaneously. There are too many opportunities to make mistakes or leave stupid loose ends. You will be learning multiple systems, multiple software setups, multiple hardware setups, and the names of many people.

Even if you have a penchant for multitasking, the level of risk this creates is not worth the reward -, not to mention the toll it can take on one's mental health.

There's no reason to onboard two jobs simultaneously. It's fucked. I recommend two months between the onboarding. Remember, you're trying to be excellent at these positions, not barely keep your head above water at each one. It may take some time to adjust to each system, and make sure you know how to organize your tasks while playing your role each day. 2-3 months is typically enough time to get embedded in the first job to get a good picture of what's expected of you and get to know the people well enough to have some leeway when dipping out of meetings or showing up late. It may also be smart to wait for a performance evaluation before stacking second and third positions. That way, you have confirmation you are crushing the one in front of you before considering others.

STRESS IS A KILLER, KILLAH

No matter what you do, prioritize your health and relationships over work. None of this shit is worth it if you lose the people who love you. If you drive them away with your obsessiveness, constantly prattling on about your OverEmployment successes, and how everyone else is stupid for not devoting that much time to salaried jobs, you'll have a lot of money and only strippers to share it with. Which is... only ok. Not great. So if you're looking for "ok," bang all the strippers. If you want "great" "remarkable" or "amazing," don't be a self-consumed dickhead about your OverEmployment endeavors.

We spend a lot of time in front of the computer, sitting at desks in awkward positions, soaking up negative ions while eating shit foods. So it's good to have a healthy diet and get some exercise.

I have an exercise regimen that is part of my daily mental cool-down. When I step away from the computer, I put on my running shoes, leash up my Shepherd, and head out for a two-mile run. It's the perfect way to clear my head and shake out the stiffness from sitting in a chair all day. /* *Sorry. The paragraph above is a total fucking lie. I just wanted to sound cool. I'm a lazy, chubby bastard. You should do that. Find your thing and enjoy a long healthy, wealthy life. I'll keep eating my Nutter Butters.*/

Chapter 5

Keep it Like a Secret

HYPOCRITICAL OATH LOAF

Why are we expected to tell our employer that we're working more than one job, and they're not likely to give us a warning when they're planning to lay us off? Shouldn't we be allowed to have a backup plan? Should we put our families at risk of losing income with no Safety-net? If you look at it in this context, the idea is absurd. We're supposed to put our lives and families at risk while employers get to choose our destinies.

When it comes to my life and my family, this is not a risk I'm willing to take, and if you call me a liar for looking out for what's important to me, then so be it. I'm perfectly willing to lie by omission when protecting my family. How often does it happen that layoffs come around right before bonus time? Fuck that. Do they lie by omission by not telling you they will rob you of your bonus money? Assholes. The hypocrisy is palpable. Sure, it may not be "telling the whole truth," but they do not need to know your life's story, nor anything else that does not directly affect your performance. So, in the schema of OverEmployment, that is your responsibility: do not allow the other jobs to cause such a struggle that you commit an egregious fuckup. Be very strict with yourself that, when switching gears between each position, that organization (and its employees) get your undivided attention for that slice of the day. Show them that respect with every moment, because every moment you are only able to try OverEmployment because of the slack they pick up during. Appreciate your coworkers, and remember you are making out like a fucking BANDIT. So, be patient and extremely conscientious when working with colleagues helping make your hustle possible.

Just remember that a company's employment policy is just that. It's their employment policy. It's not your employment policy. So outside of a violation of an NDA or non-compete, when you leave that job, that policy is their business, not yours. It doesn't go with you where you go. Make sure to look through all the papers you signed to avoid accidentally breaching your contract during OverEmployment! This should be done at the beginning, as mentioned earlier in sections 1 and 2.

If you challenge an employment policy while working for a company, that's your right.

It's their choice to accept your challenge or let you go.

As a general rule, you don't want to quit a job; make them fire you. But your exit strategy can include ways to leave the job with compensation for PTO. First, you want to agree with the company on exit terms before getting fired. Then, if you get fired, you can at least try to get severance pay. In the world of OverEmployment, getting fired is no big deal, so long as it is contained. Moving on from position to position will likely be a part of many OverEmployment practitioners.

DON'T HATE THE PLAYER

When people see that you're banking, they will inevitably ask you what you do. The short and sweet answer is, "I'm a consultant." You can tell them that you work with many clients in the tech industry or even what you do specifically. For example, "I'm a technology consultant and work with several clients." That's an honest answer and doesn't give away too much. If they ask you about the clients, use nicknames.

SHUT THE FUCK UP

When you've discovered a way to make much more money than most people will ever know, it'll be hard not to brag. It's a natural part of the ego. You'll want to show off your knowledge, and present your fancy OverEmployment plan like a sports car with suicide doors. It.may sound like common sense, but this is an easy way to get caught. So, be vigilant of what you're telling people, and resist the urge to brag even though you deserve to.

If there is any exception to this rule, and I'm not saying this is a good idea, you can tell your partner if you must. For example, legally married, you can tell your partner because they have skin in the game. However, don't tell them anything if you are just dating someone. You are a "consultant." Leave it at that. Why? Well, there's a good possibility the relationship will end badly /*as they usually do*/, and they might want revenge. Also, if they know you're working two jobs, they can easily screw you. So keep your mouth shut and your bank account flush.

DON'T POST SHIT

Research done by Facebook showed that there are only three degrees of separation between any two people on Facebook. Ain't that some shit? Because of social media, we no longer have six degrees of separation.

This is a tough one for most people. Not letting work information get out to your coworkers or HR people doing a little background check on you is critical.

- Start with a Google search to see what is out there about your work history.
- Hibernate or delete your LinkedIn presence.
- Set social media accounts to super private privacy settings or simply delete them.

By hibernating your LinkedIn account, you will avoid leaking any information about where or who you work with. It can be a little awkward when your new coworkers ask why you haven't added them on LinkedIn yet. I keep my LinkedIn account hibernated and use the excuse that I just get sick of constant notifications. In truth, I don't use LinkedIn much at all, so the reason is valid. The truth is the best lie.

We want to keep as many degrees of separation between us and anyone related to our jobs as possible. That's why you need to set all your privacy settings on Facebook /*or any other social media account*/ to the highest level of privacy. And, never post anything about work. Ideally, you will make it simple and shut down any mention of work on all your social media accounts.

WE'RE USING NICKNAMES

This tip is kind of silly, but it can save you some pain in the long run. Instead of using the actual names of the companies you're working for, make up nicknames for them. That way, when you're talking about an employer, you're not divulging information that could allow someone who overhears to track down that employer to report you. This can apply to in-person conversations and online conversations.

This little trick is even good for friends and family.

CURIOSITY KILLS YOUR ASS

When your friends are at your house and see your crazy tech setup and all your new gear, they will ask questions. Just remember you're a consultant, and you do work for different companies that often have additional security requirements, software setups, VPNs, etc. This is why you have multiple setups.

SNITCHES GET STITCHES

Don't go snitching on others who are OverEmployed. Whether you choose OverEmployment or not, how others make their money is none of your business.

Chapter 6

Eye On The Exit

KNOW WHEN TO GTFO

An exit strategy goes along with your goal when you reach your goal and need a plan to exit. But an exit strategy can also help you when something like a reprimand comes up. Or you're dealing with a micromanager, "I'm Going To Need Those TPS Reports ASAP. So, If You Could Do That, That'd Be Greaaaaat." You don't need Bill Lumberg up your ass all the time, affecting your other jobs. Time to go. Stop producing. Stop going to meetings. Get a severance check and move on. Be like water with your second and third positions. They are gravy anyways; you don't need them, so cut your losses and dip when the position becomes untenable to balance with your other responsibilities.

DON'T HATE THE PLAYA, HATE THE GAME

Whatever you do, don't fall in love with a job. When you're in love, you lose all ability to reason. Don't fool yourself into thinking that the people you're working for have your best interests in mind; they don't love you, so you shouldn't love them back. We're out to make a buck, not to make friends. If you start making decisions like they are your friends, not your coworkers, they're going to end up pissed at you, eyes raised thinking you were delusional or just plain stupid.

After you make money, you can fall in love with the job, make friends, stay there for the rest of your life, be super happy, and never get laid off because they love you so much. But don't take the risk until you have that million dollars in your bank account. Keep people at arm's length; don't fool yourself into believing that you have the perfect situation because it could end at any moment. And, when it does, you need to be emotionally ready to move on.

DON'T BE A QUITTER

It can be humiliating to get yourself fired, but there's never a reason to quit a job. If it's time to leave, slowly degrade your work's quality or work less and less. Then, create reasons for them to start the process of letting you go. If it starts to look like they're going to put you through PIP, then negotiate an exit plan with your employer by telling them you're willing to leave if they pay you severance. This method can give you a couple of extra months of pay as you start your new job. You can also negotiate payment for paid time off /*PTO*/ that has not been used. If you quit, you get nothing. Either way, remember when you are getting fired it is from your second or third position. The entire endeavor was a bit of an experiment, so do not fret if things do not immediately bounce back after a firing. Simply collect your thoughts, and focus on stabilizing your core position.

DEAD MAN WALKING

"Don't let yourself get attached to anything you are not willing to walk out on in 30 seconds flat if you feel the heat around the corner."

— Robert De Niro, Heat, 1995

Always assume that today will be your last day and prepare accordingly. Your "go bag" needs to include cloud-backed personal records, notes, CYA documentation, and any job-related information you plan to take with you. In addition, make sure you have an alternate health insurance plan engaged. Finally, update everything in your cloud storage regularly. Then, when it does happen, take the opportunity to enjoy some time off on a beach in Hawaii, funded by your severance package. If you are planning on jumping ship, reread this section before you do! It will ensure max severance pay and a smooth transition to your next OverEmployment opportunity.

GET PAID

If you are given a negative performance review, and you're going to be put on a PIP, the jig is up. It's time to grab your shit and head for the door. But, first, coast for a month while they put the plan in place, and you hold a few more paychecks. You can also use this time to interview for more jobs. Remember, this is your burner job, so you don't need it as long as you have job one and job zero is on your resume for work history. Then you can ask for severance and tell them they can save the expense of putting you through a PIP when you both know it's not going to work out. In the end, it's not personal for either side. The best option financially for both parties will be the easiest solution to agree upon.

FUCK GOODBYES

Virtual farewell lunches are stupid and create the opportunity for you to be presented with questions that you might not easily be able to answer. People will ask you over and over again what you're going to do next. Do yourself a favor and skip it altogether. Make up an excuse for why you can't be there and save yourself the pain of an awkward situation. If you can't think of a better reason, just claim to have covid and tell them to fuck off.

Conclusion

The pandemic changed a lot in the world. One of the significant changes in the United States was that everyone went home to work. This paradigm shift created perfect conditions for technology workers to test out OverEmployment. Now, it's never been easier to hold multiple jobs simultaneously because working from home is the accepted norm in many companies. The opportunity to make two or three times the average salary has proved irresistible for many highly-skilled technology workers.

The movement is backed by the sentiment that workers should be paid for their ability to produce and the intellectual property they possess from years of learning their craft. Corporations are out to grab as much money as possible. Now technology workers are approaching their employment as their own business to cash in.

Who knows how long the conditions will support this trend? The recession may cause a more fractured job market and eliminate some technology jobs that are readily available today. The slow return to a career in the office mindset may impact the opportunities for multiple remote jobs. Once pandemic survival mode has ended, employers may have less tolerance for workers who have reduced in-person interaction with their bosses and co-workers.

It's hard to imagine knowledge workers getting blocked from OverEmployment as long as the economy strongly favors the workers. If your goal is to make $1,000,000 and retire to Amsterdam, you only need the next five years to get it done. So get off your ass and go get what you are worth.

References

"12 Rules For Working Two Remote Jobs," https://overemployed.com/, Overemployed Guild, Anonymous, 2022

"Now, out of the daily eye of managers, people are taking on additional, secret jobs. What could go wrong?" https://www.bbc.com/worklife/article/20210927-the-overemployed-workers-juggling-remote-jobs, Bryan Lufkin, September 28th, 2021

"How OverEmployment Movement Is Impacting Technology Industry," https://www.itprotoday.com/career-development/how-overemployment-movement-impacting-it-industry, Christopher Tozzi, Jun 16, 2022

"10 Commandments Of OE," https://overemployed.com/, Overemployed Guild, Anonymous, 2022

"Two In-Person Jobs – The Original OE," https://overemployed.com/story-two-in-person-jobs-the-original-oe/, Overemployed Guild, Anonymous, 2022

Index

Introduction 1
   WTF IS OVEREMPLOYED? 3
   HAVE THE POWER HE-MAN 7
   REVENGE OF THE NERD 11
   THE BIG BUCKS 13
   INSIDER SECRETS 17

Chapter 1 18
   Getting The Jobs 18
   MISE EN SCÈNE 19
   BE READY FOR ANYTHING 23
   YOU ARE A BUSINESS 25
   JOB TWO INTERVIEW 26
   A BACKUP RESUME 28
   STARTUPS OR BOOMERS 29
   OFFSHORE OUTSIDER 31
   TIME TIME ZONES 35
   CHECKING YOUR RAP SHEET 36
   YOU CAN FREEZE YOUR RECORDS ... 38
   PICK A DAMN JOB 39
   DON'T SIGN SHIT 40

Chapter 2 42
   Manage The Jobs 42
   GET ON BOARD 42
   BAD SECURITY 42
   MF'n MFA 43

CROSS-CONTAMINATION 44
CAMERAS OFF 45
ASS KISSER 45
DUH 46
FUCKING INTERNET 47
TO-DO TO-DON'T 48

Chapter 3 50
Maximize Efficiency 50
DO AS LITTLE AS POSSIBLE 50
DEEP BRAIN 51
YODA SHIT 52
MEDIOCRACY 54
STAY ON TARGET 55
I GOT BETTER SHIT TO DO 56
ROBO CALENDAR 58
SKIP THAT SHIT 59

Chapter 4 61
Save Your Sanity 61
WHAT THE HELL DO YOU WANT? 61
FORGET IT 62
FUCK NO, I WON'T GO 63
MAKE technology RAIN 65
GET A LITTLE HELP 66
HABITUAL LINE STEPPERS 67
SLOW YOUR ROLL 69
STRESS IS A KILLER, KILLAH 71

Chapter 5 73
Keep it Like a Secret 73

HYPOCRITICAL OATH LOAF 73
DON"T HATE THE PLAYER 76
SHUT THE FUCK UP 77
DON"T POST SHIT 78
WE'RE USING NICKNAMES 80
CURIOSITY KILLS YOUR ASS 81
SNITCHES GET STITCHES 81

Chapter 6 82

Eye On The Exit 82

KNOW WHEN TO GTFO 82
DON"T HATE THE PLAYA, HATE THE GAME
.... 83
DON"T BE A QUITTER 84
DEAD MAN WALKING 85
GET PAID 86
FUCK GOODBYES 87

Conclusion 88
References 91

www.ingramcontent.com/pod-product-compliance
Lightning Source LLC
Chambersburg PA
CBHW050245220526
45465CB00002B/551